Richard Cobden

Russia, Turkey, and England

Richard Cobden

Russia, Turkey, and England

ISBN/EAN: 9783337299231

Printed in Europe, USA, Canada, Australia, Japan

Cover: Foto ©ninafisch / pixelio.de

More available books at **www.hansebooks.com**

BY

RICHARD COBDEN.

Reprinted from "THE POLITICAL WRITINGS OF RICHARD COBDEN."

FREE TRADE·PEACE·GOODWILL AMONG NATIONS

Cobden Club

CASSELL PETTER & GALPIN:

LONDON, PARIS & NEW YORK.

1876.

PREFATORY NOTE.

THE following pamphlet, which originally appeared in 1836, is re-published by the Committee of the COBDEN CLUB, in the belief that it will be read with fresh interest by the light of recent events. Had Mr. Cobden lived to revise it, after the lapse of forty years, it is probable he might have seen fit to re-consider certain passages or expressions, but there is no reason to suppose that he would have modified in any essential respect the principles of foreign policy which are here so clearly laid down.

RUSSIA, TURKEY, AND ENGLAND.

IT has been somewhere remarked that in former times some false alarms usually preceded or accompanied a new war. Thus, in 1792, Mr. Saunderson, then Lord Mayor, and soon afterwards made a Baronet, got up in his place in the House of Commons, and declared that he knew of a plot to surprise the Tower of London : all England was thrown into a fear of the Jacobins, and the anti-Jacobin war soon afterwards followed ; but of the conspiracy to seize the Tower, not another word was heard. Again, at the close of the short peace, or, more properly speaking, the *truce* of Amiens, it was alleged, in all the public prints, and subsequently inserted in the declaration of war, that Bonaparte had armies ready to invade England ; and, in proof, it was adduced that instructions had been given to the French diplomatic and commercial agents to take surveys and soundings of our coasts and harbours.* The people, thus deluded

* " When once Persia fell under the yoke of Russia, one great obstacle to the acquirement of that which constituted our possessions in the East

into an anti-Bonaparte war, forgot that many different
surveys of every part of our coast, and of every harbour
in the British dominions, might have been purchased for
a few shillings at every hydrographer's or chart-seller's ;
and that no foreigner, by years of study, could have
added an iota to the information contained in the various
pilot-books then used in the different channels. We live
in other times ; but still the constitution of our government, which gives to the Court the power of declaring
war, and to the Commons the privilege of providing for
its expenses, remains the same ; and, however we may
be verging upon a more secure era, we confess we think
there is sufficient ground in the predominant influence
which an aristocracy, essentially warlike, exercises at
this moment in the Ministry, to warn our readers and
the public against the passion for a foolish war, with
which the minds of the people have been latterly very
industriously inflamed. We do not charge the noble
Lords who form the great majority in the Cabinet with
a design to stimulate the country to demand hostilities
with Russia ; the policy of the Ministry may probably
have stopped far short of that, and aimed only at ac-
complishing an augmentation of the army or navy.
Certain it is, however, that *one active mind* * has, during
the last two years, materially influenced the tone of
several of the newspapers of this kingdom, in reference
to the affairs of Russia and Turkey, and incessantly
roused public opinion, through every accessible channel
of the periodical press, against the former and in favour
of the latter nation ; certain it is, moreover, that this

would be removed. He hoped that its success would be impossible—it was
at least problematical; but this, at all events, was in no degree doubtful, that
the matter was very seriously entertained at St. Petersburg. *In the War-
office there, maps and plans, drawn expressly for the purpose, were deposited,
showing not only the practicability of such a scheme of aggrandisement, but the
various modes in which it might be best carried into effect, and the way the
several military stations necessary for the purpose might be established."*—
Lord Dudley Stuart's Speech, House of Commons, Feb. 19, 1836.

* [Mr. David Urquhart.]

individual, if not previously an agent of the Government, has latterly become so, by being appointed to a diplomatic post in our embassy at Constantinople.* How far this indefatigable spirit has been successful in his design to diffuse a feeling of terror and a spirit of hatred towards Russia in the public mind, may be ascertained by any one who will take the trouble to sound the opinions of his next neighbour upon the subject, whom, it is ten to one, he will find an alarmist about the subtlety of Pozzo di Borgo, the cruelty of the Czar, and the barbarism of the Russians. He most likely will find him to possess but vague feelings of apprehension, and very little exactness of knowledge upon the subject; he will not know, perhaps, precisely, whether the province of Moldavia be on the right or the left bank of the Danube, or whether the Balkan and the ancient Hæmus be an identical range of mountains; he will have but an indistinct acquaintance with the geography of Asia Minor, and probably confound the Bosphorus with the Dardanelles: but still he shall be profoundly alarmed at the encroachments of Russia in those quarters, and quite willing to go to war to prevent them. Such, we gravely assert, is the feeling, and such are the opinions, of the great majority of those who take their doctrines from some of the newspapers at this moment, upon the question of Russian aggrandisement. Believing that the fate of Turkey, and the designs of her great northern neighbour, are by no means matters that affect the interests of England so vitally as some writers imagine, we are yet more directly opposed to them, by entertaining a conviction that, even if the worst of their forebodings were to arrive—if even Russia were to subjugate Turkey—England would gain rather than suffer by the event. In order to state our views fairly upon this interesting and difficult question, it will be necessary for us to glance, hastily, at the past history and

* We state these facts from personal knowledge.

the present condition, as respects the government and resources, of the two empires; and then, having assumed that Turkey had fallen a prey to the ambition of Russia, we will weigh the probable consequences of, and meet the possible objections to, such an event.

But, before entering upon our task, we would disavow all intention of advocating the cause of Russian violence and aggression. It can only be necessary to say thus much at the outset of this pamphlet, in order to prevent the reader from anticipating our design with an undue prepossession respecting our motives; for the whole spirit and purpose of the following pages will show that we are hostile to the government of St. Petersburg, and to every principle of its foreign and domestic policy. Our sympathies flow, altogether, towards those free institutions which are favourable to the peace, wealth, education, and happiness of mankind.

In comparing the Turkish government with that of Russia, however, it will be found that the latter is immeasurably the superior in its laws and institutions; and if, in the remarks which we shall have occasion to make, we should appear to bestow commendations upon that northern people, we entreat that the reader will consider us to be only speaking in comparison with its more barbarous and despotic Mahometan neighbour, and not from any abstract predilection in favour of the Russian nation. Again, whilst we argue that we should, in all probability, benefit by the subjugation of Turkey by Russia, we do not attempt to justify, or even to palliate, the forcible spoliation of its territory: still less do we advocate the intervention of the English government, for the purpose of promoting such a conquest. Our sole object is to persuade the public that the wisest policy for England is to take no part in those remote quarrels. To accomplish this end we will endeavour to examine every distinct source of danger which the advocates for our interference in the affairs of states a thousand miles distant, adduce as arguments in defence of their policy.   We shall claim the right of putting the question entirely upon a footing of self-interest.   We do not, for a moment, imagine that it is necessary for us to show that we are not called upon to preserve the peace and good order of the entire world.   Indeed, those writers and speakers who argue in favour of our intervention in the affairs of Russia and Turkey, invariably do so upon the pretence that our commerce, our colonies, or our national existence are endangered by the encroachments of the former empire.   We trust the futility of such fears will be shown by the following appeal to reason, experience, and facts.

The Turks, a race of the Tartars of Asia, conquered Constantinople in 1453.   In the succeeding century, this people struck terror into all Europe by their conquests.   They subdued Egypt, the Barbary States, and all the Arabian coasts on the Red Sea.   In Europe, they conquered the Crimea and the countries along the Danube ; they overran Hungary and Transylvania, and repeatedly laid siege to Vienna.   At sea, notwithstanding the gallant resistance of the Venetians, they subdued Rhodes, Cyprus, and all the Greek islands. Down to our own time the Turks governed a territory so vast and fertile that, in ancient ages, it comprised Egypt, Phœnicia, Syria, Greece, Carthage, Thrace, Pontus, Bithynia, Cappadocia, Epirus, and Armenia, besides other less renowned empires.   From three of these states went forth, at various epochs, conquerors who vanquished and subjected the then entire known world.   The present lamentable condition of this fine territory, so renowned in former times, arises from no change in the seasons, or defalcation of nature.   It still stretches from 34 to 48 deg. north, within the temperate zone, and upon the same parallels of latitudes as Spain, France, and all the best portion of the United States.   "Mount Hæmus," says Malte Brun, " is still covered with verdant forests ; the plains of Thrace, Macedonia, and Thessaly yield abundant and easy harvests to the husbandman ; a thousand ports and a thousand gulfs are observed on the coasts, peninsulas, and islands. The calm billows of these tranquil seas still bathe the base of mountains covered with vines and olive-trees. But the populous and numerous towns mentioned by ancient writers have been changed into deserts beneath a despotic government." All the authorities upon this country assure us that the soil of many parts of Turkey is more fruitful than the richest plains of Sicily. When grazed by the rudest plough, it yields a more abundant harvest than the finest fields between the Eure and the Loire, ·the granary of France. Mines of silver, copper, and iron are still existing, and salt abounds in the country. Cotton. tobacco, and silk might be made the staple exports of this region, and their culture admits of almost unlimited extension throughout the Turkish territory ; whilst some of the native wines are equal to those of Burgundy. Almost every species of tree flourishes in European Turkey. The heights of the Danube are clad with apple, pine, cherry, and apricot trees ; whole forests of these may be seen in Wallachia ; and they cover the hills of Thrace, Macedonia, and Epirus. The olive, orange, mastic, fig, pomegranate—the laurel, myrtle, and nearly all the beautiful and aromatic shrubs and plants—are natural to this soil. Nor are the animal productions less valuable than those of vegetable life. The finest horses have been drawn from this quarter, to improve the breeds of Western Europe ; and the rich pastures of European Turkey are, probably, the best adapted in the world for rearing the largest growths of cattle and sheep.

That, in a region so highly favoured, the population should have retrograded, whilst surrounded by abundance ; that its wealth and industry should have been annihilated ; and that commerce should be banished from those rivers and harbours that first called it into existence—must be accounted for by remembering that the finest soil, the most genial climate, or the brightest intellectual and physical gifts of human nature, are as nothing, when subjected to the benumbing influences of the government of Constantinople. It is necessary to refer to the religion and the maxims of its professors, which constitute all that serves as a substitute for law with this Mahometan people, if we would know the causes why ignorance, barbarism, and poverty now overspread the fairest lands of Asia and Europe. The Turks profess, as is well known, the most bigoted and intolerant branch of the Mahometan faith ; they regard with equal detestation the Persian Shiite and the follower of Christ ; nay, the more zealous amongst their doctors contend that it is as meritorious to slay one Shiite as twenty Christians. Their colleges, or madresses, teach nothing but the Mahometan theology ; many years being spent in mastering such knotty points as, *whether the feet should be washed at rising, or only rubbed with the dry hand.* As the orthodox Turk, of whatever rank, is taught to despise all other fields of learning than the Koran, under the belief that Mahomet has, in that sacred book, recorded all that his faithful followers are required to know—it follows, of course, that he is religiously ignorant of all that forms the education of a Frenchman, German, or Italian ; he knows nothing of the countries beyond the bounds of the Sultan's dominions. The Turks (unlike the liberal Persians, who have made some advances in science) are unacquainted with the uses of the commonest scientific instruments, which are exhibited to them by travellers just as we do to amuse children. Notwithstanding that this people have been for nearly four centuries in absolute possession of all the noblest remains of ancient art, they have evinced no taste for architecture or sculpture, whilst painting and music are equally unknown to them. Nor have they been less careless about the preservation of ancient, than the creation of modern works of labour and ingenuity. They found, at the conquest of the eastern empire, splendid and substantial public and private edifices, which have been barbarously destroyed, or allowed to crumble beneath the hand of time; and huts of wood, compared by travellers to large boxes* standing in rows with their lids open upon hinges, compose the streets of modern Constantinople and other large cities. Bridges, aqueducts, and harbours, the precious and durable donations of remote, yet more enlightened generations, have all suffered a like fate; and the roads, even in the vicinity of the capital, which in former ages maintained an unrivalled celebrity, are described, by the last tourist,† to be now in so broken and neglected a state as to present a barrier against the progress of artillery as complete as though it had been designed by an engineer for that purpose.

The cause of all this decay is ascribed to the genius of the Turkish Government—a fierce, unmitigated military despotism—allied with the fanaticism of a brutalising religion, which teaches its followers to rely solely on the sword, and to disdain all improvement and labour. The Sultan, who is the vicegerent of the Prophet, holds both temporal and spiritual authority over his followers; and this enables him to sway the lives and destinies of the people, with an absoluteness greater than was ever enjoyed by any tyrant of ancient times; unchecked, too, by the growth of cities, the increase of knowledge, or the accumulation of wealth—all which are alike incompatible with the present government of the country. Every man, who is invested with absolute power, is at liberty to delegate his power unimpaired to another: the Sultan is the vicegerent of the Prophet; every Pasha is a representative of the Sultan; and every soldier who carries an order, the representative of the Pasha. The situations of Pasha and Cadi, or judge, are all given to the highest bidders, who are removable at will, and, of course, take care to indemnify themselves at the expense of the governed. "It is a fact of public notoriety," says

* Willis—"Pencillings by the Way."
† Quin—"Voyage down the Danube."

Thornton,* " that governments of every description are
openly sold at the Porte ; they are held for the term of
one year only, and, at the ensuing *bairam*, the leases
must be renewed or transferred to a less parsimonious
competitor.   In the public registers, the precise value of
every important post under government is recorded ; and
the regular remittance of the taxes and tribute is the
only acknowledged criterion of upright administration."
It is a fundamental principle that all the property conquered by the Turks belongs to the Sultan.   Hence the
Christians are accounted the slaves of the conqueror, and
they are only allowed to live by paying a heavy tribute,
the receipt for which bears that it is the ransom of their
heads !

Probably, in nothing has this people been more un-
duly represented than in the praises which have been
bestowed on their unrestricted principles of trade.   The
Turk knows nothing, and cares as little, about freedom
of commerce ; he disdains trade himself, and despises it
in others ; and, if he has failed to imitate more civilised
(though, certainly, in this point of view, not wiser) nations,
by fortifying his coasts with custom-houses, it is certainly
from no wise principle of taxation, but simply because
such a circuitous method of fiscal exaction would be far
too complicated and wearisome for the minds of Ottoman
governors, who prefer the simpler mode of raising a
revenue by the direct extortion of the Pasha or the Aga.
Far from favouring the extension of commerce, one great
cause of the present barbarism and the past unhappy
condition of Turkey, is to be found in the aversion and
contempt which its people bear for trade.   " The Jews,"
says Hadji-Khalfa, the Turkish writer, in speaking of
Salonica, " employ many workmen in their different
manufactories—support a number of schools, in which
there are not fewer than two hundred masters.   The
caravans that travel from Salonica to Semlin, Vienna,

* " Present State of Turkey."

and Leipsig, are loaded with cotton, tobacco, carpets, and leather. It is a shame," continues the orthodox Hadji-Khalfa, "that so many Jews are allowed to remain in Salonica ; the excitement thus given to trade is apt to blind true believers." The fate of those vast and rich tracts bordering upon the Black Sea and its tributary rivers, affords ample proof that the genius of Mahometanism is inimical to the interests of commerce and agriculture. The trade carried on by the ancients upon the shores of the Euxine was very considerable, and gave life and wealth to several populous cities mentioned in history. In more modern times the Genoese formed establishments upon the coasts of the Black Sea, and they took the lead in navigating those waters down to the fifteenth century. At the taking of Constantinople, the Turks closed the Black Sea against the ships of Europe ; and from that time its navigation was lost to the commerce of the world for a period of more than three centuries.

By the treaty of Kanardgi, in 1774, the ships of Russia were allowed to pass the Bosphorus ; other countries soon afterwards obtained similar privileges ; some restrictions, which it was still attempted to keep up, were removed by the treaty between the Russians and Turks in 1829 ; and the Black Sea is now, for commercial purposes, as open as the Mediterranean. The importance of this vast extension of commercial navigation cannot, at present, be fully appreciated, owing to the unfortunate condition of the population which inhabits those regions. Some idea may, however, be formed of the extent and probable importance of those great rivers which fall into the Black Sea, by the following estimate furnished by Malte Brun :—

If all the rivers in Europe be as   1.COO
Those which flow into the Black Sea,   0.273
     „   „   Mediterranean,   0.144

Of all the features belonging to the Turkish national character, there is none less favourable than that which relates to the neglect and contempt with which that people has invariably treated affairs of trade. Whether it be owing to that dogma of their creed which forbids the receiving interest for money, or to that other familiar text of the Koran, which says, "There is but one law, and that forbids all communication with infidels;" certain it is that such an example as a Turkish merchant transacting matters of commerce with a foreign trader was scarcely ever known in that country. This is an anomaly the more striking when we refer to other countries, less advantageously situated, as, for instance, China, where trade has acquired an importance, and is conducted on a system the growth of ages of good government, and of a like period of patient industry in the people. Nothing but a tyrannical despotism, at once sanguinary and lawless, could have had the effect of repelling commerce from the superb harbour of Constantinople; but, alas! the thousand ships which might find secure anchorage there would seek in vain for the rich freights of silk, cotton, and wool, which ought to await their coming : such is the character of its people and rulers, that no native capitalists have ever been emboldened to accumulate a store of merchandise to tempt the rapacity of the Sultan ; and vessels which trade to Constantinople have frequently occasion to go to Salonica, Smyrna, or some other port, for return cargoes.

Before we turn away from this hasty and assuredly not very pleasing glance at the Ottoman nation, it would be uncandid if we omitted to notice the imputed virtues of the Turks ; foremost amongst which stands charity— a quality enjoined to all true believers by the words of Mahomet, and which includes within its operation the inferior animals. They are reputed to be honourable in their dealings, and faithful to their words—characteristics of the haughty masters, as lying and chicane are natural to the slave. The Turks are forbidden the use of wine ; but, then, they console themselves by substituting the

B

eternal coffee, tobacco, and opium, and by other sensual indulgences.

"We turn," in the words of a great writer, "from the soil of barbarism and the crescent, to a country whose inhabitants participate in the blessings of Christianity and European civilization."

Russia comprises one-half of Europe, one-third of Asia, and a portion of America ; and includes within its bounds nearly sixty millions, or a sixteenth portion of the human race. Its territory stretches, in length, from the Black Sea to the confines of Upper Canada ; and from the border of China to the Arctic Sea, in width. The stupendous size of the Russian empire has excited the wonder and alarm of timid writers, who forget that " it is an identity of language, habits, and character, and not the soil or the name of a master, which constitutes a great and powerful nation." Ruling over eighty different nations or tribes, the autocrat of all the Russias claims the allegiance of people of every variety of race, tongue, and religion. Were it possible to transport to one common centre of his empire the gay opera lounger of St. Petersburg, habited in the Parisian mode ; the fierce Bashkir of the Ural Mountain, clad in rude armour, and armed with bow and arrows; the Crimean, with his camel, from the southern steppes ; and the Esquimaux, who traverses with his dogs the frozen regions of the north—these fellow-subjects of one potentate would encounter each other with all the surprise and ignorance of individuals meeting from England, China, Peru, and New Holland ; *nor would the time or expense incurred in the journey be greater in the latter than the former interview.* It must be obvious to every reflecting mind that vast deductions must be made from the written and statistical resources of a nation possessing no unison of religious or political feeling, when put in competition with other empires, identified in faith, language, and national characteristics. The popular mind has been, however, greatly misled by many writers on the Russian empire, who have sought to impress their readers with the idea of the overwhelming size of its territory, and who have, at the same time, wilfully or negligently omitted to mention other facts, which, if taken in connection, serve to render that very magnitude of surface a source of weakness rather than power. We are furnished by Malte Brun with some tables of the relative densities of the population of the European empires, which will help to illustrate our views upon this subject, and from which we give an extract :—

	Inhabitants.
Russia, for each square league . .	181
Prussia	792
France	1,063
England	1,457

Now, the same law applies to communities as to physics—in proportion as you condense you strengthen, and as you draw out you weaken bodies : and, according to this rule, the above table, which makes Prussia more than four times as closely peopled as Russia, would, bearing in mind the advantages of her denser population, give to the former power an equality of might with her unwieldy neighbour, which we have no doubt, is quite consistent with the truth ; whilst the same tabular test, if applied to Russia, France, and England, would assign much the greater share of power to the two latter nations; which experience has demonstrated to be the fact. Here, then, we have the means of exemplifying, by a very simple appeal to figures (ever the best reasoning weapons), how the vastness of territory of the Russians is the cause of debility rather than of strength. It would be a trite illustration of a self-evident truism if we were to adduce, as a proof of our argument, the practice in military tactics. What general ever dreamed of scattering his troops, by way of increasing their power ? Bonaparte gained his terrible battles by manœuvering great masses of men in smaller limits than any preceding commanders.

But the same geographer supplies us with a gra-
duated scale of the relative taxation of these countries,
which affords a yet more convincing proof of the disad-
vantageous position of Russia.

Russia, each inhabitant contributes to government.	.	.	.	£0	11	8
Prussia .	.	.	.	.	0	17	6
France .	.	.	.	.	1	8	4
England.	.	.	.	.	3	13	5

Now, assuming, as we may safely do, that these
governments draw the utmost possible revenue from
their subjects, what a disproportion here is between the
wealth of the closely-peopled Britain, and the poverty
of the scantily populated Russia! We find, too, that
the gradation of wealth is in the direct proportion to the
density of the inhabitants of the four countries. Here,
then, we have a double source of weakness for Russia,
which would operate in a duplicate ratio to her dis-
advantage, in case that nation were plunged into a
war with either of those other states; for, whilst her
armies must necessarily be mustered from greater
distances, at proportionate cost, and with less ability
on her part to bear those charges, her rivals would
possess troops more compactly positioned, and, at the
same time, the greater means of transporting them—
in a word, the one party would require the funds, and
not possess them, whilst the other would, comparatively
speaking, have the money, and not want it. A necessary
evil attends the wide-spread character of the population
of Russia, in the absence of those large towns which
serve as centres of intelligence and nurses of civilization
in other countries. Thus, in those vast regions, we have
the cities of

Petersburgh, with a population of	.	.	305 000
Moscow	.	.	.	.	.	.	190,000
Warsaw	.	.	.	.	.	.	117,000
Kasan .	.	.	.	.	.	.	50,000
Kiow .	.	.	.	.	.	.	40,000

whilst we find the remainder of the large places on the

map of Russia to be only, in size, upon a par with the third-rate towns of England. That in a country of such vast extent, and comprising sixty millions of people, and where so few populous cities exist, the great mass of the inhabitants are living in poverty, ignorance, and barbarism, scarcely rising above a state of nature, must be apparent. Tribes of Cossacks and of Tartars, wandering over the low countries of Caucasia, own a formal allegiance to Russia. Other hordes, dignified by the alarmist writers on the subject of Russian greatness, with the title of *nations*—such as the Circassians, the Georgians, the Mingrelians, with more than thirty other tribes, some Christian, others Mahometan, or of a mixed creed, occupying the mountainous regions of the Caucasus— are wholly or partially subdued to the dominion of the Czar. These fierce tribes are addicted to all the rude habits of savages ; they live by the chase, or the cultivation of a little millet ; they commit barbarous outrages, and buy and sell each other for slaves—often disposing of their own children, brothers, and sisters, to the Turks. Against these refractory and half-subdued neighbours, the Russians are compelled to keep fortresses along the frontier.

If we pass to northern Russia, we find the Samoiedes, a people enduring nearly six months of perpetual night, and enjoying, in requital, a day of two months ; with them, corn is sown, ripened, and reaped, in sixty days. In the governments of Wologda, Archangel, and Olonetz (for even in this almost uninhabitable region man has established his ministerial arrangements and political divisions) the climate is of such a nature that human industry can hardly contend against the elements, and the scanty produce of his labour enables the husbandman scarcely to protract a painful and sometimes precarious existence. Trees disappear on the sterile plains—the plants are stunted—corn withers—the marshy meadows are covered with rushes and mosses—and the whole of vegetable nature proclaims the vicinity of the Pole.

Over these desolate wastes, a traveller might journey five hundred miles, and not encounter one solitary human habitation. The government or province of Orenburg is larger than the entire kingdom of Prussia, and yet contains only a population of one million souls!

There are, however, vast districts—as, for example, the whole of Little Russia, and the Ukraine—of fertile territory, equal in richness to any part of Europe ; and it has been estimated that Russia contains more than 750,000 square miles of land, of a quality not inferior to the best portions of Germany, and upon which a population of two hundred millions of people might find subsistence. Here, then, is the field upon which the energies of the government and the industry of its subjects should be, for the next century, exclusively devoted ; and if the best interests of Russia were understood—or if its government would attain to that actual power which ignorant writers proclaim for it in the possession of boundless wastes and impenetrable forests—she should cease the wars of the sword, and begin the battle with the wilderness, by constructing railroads, building bridges, deepening rivers; by fostering the accumulation of capital, the growth of cities, and the increase of civilization and freedom. *These are the only sources of power and wealth in an age of improvement ;* and until Russia, like America, draws from her plains, mountains, and rivers, those resources which can be developed only by patient labour— vain are her boasts of geographical extent. As well might the inhabitants of the United States vaunt of their unexplored possessions west of the Rocky Mountains, or England plume herself upon the desert tracts of New Holland.

If such be the true interests of Russia, it will be admitted, then, that the conquest of those extensive and almost depopulated regions now withering under the government of the Sultan, would only be a wider departure from this enlightened policy. Assuming that such a conquest had taken place, it follows that the population of the Russian empire would become still more diversified in character and of a yet more heterogeneous nature ; whilst it, at the same time, would diffuse itself over a far wider surface of territory ; and, if the arguments which we have offered are founded in reason, then the first effects of all this must be, that Russia would, herself, be weakened by this still greater distension of her dominion. What, then, becomes of our apprehensions about the safety of India, or the possession of the Ionian Islands— the freedom of the Mediterranean—our maritime supremacy—or the thousand other dangers with which we are threatened as the immediate consequence of the possession of Constantinople by the Russians ?

If we would form a fair estimate of the probable results of that event, we ought to glance, for a moment, at the conduct of the same people under somewhat similar circumstances in another quarter. The policy pursued by Russia on the Gulf of Finland (where St. Petersburgh arose, like an exhalation from the marshes of the Neva), when those districts were wrested, by its founder, from the maniac Charles XII., would, we have a right to assume, be imitated by the same nation on the shores of the Bosphorus. Let us here pause to do homage to that noblest example of history, far surpassing the exploits of Alexander or Napoleon—that sublime act of devotion at the shrine of commerce and civilization, offered by Peter the Great, who, to instruct his subjects in the science of navigation and the art of ship-building, voluntarily descended from a throne, where he was surrounded by the pomp and splendour of a great potentate, and became a menial workman in the dockyards of Saardam and Deptford ! We vindicate not his crimes or his vices —the common attributes of the condition of society in which he lived ; his cruelty was but the natural fruit of irresponsible power in savage life ; and his acts of grossness and intemperance were regarded, by the nation, as honourable exploits : but the genius that enabled him to penetrate the thick clouds of prejudice and ignorance which enveloped his people, and to perceive, afar off, the power which civilization and commerce confer upon nations, was the offspring of his own unaided spirit, and will ever be worthy of peculiar honour at the hands of the historian. Everybody knows under what trying disadvantages this metropolis, planted in the midst of unhealthy and barren marshes, and in a latitude that, by the ancients, was placed beyond the limits of civilization, sprung from the hands of its founder, and stood forth the most wonderful phenomenon of the 18th century. At present this capital, which contains upwards of 300,000 inhabitants, and is termed, from the splendour of its public buildings, a city of palaces, can boast of scientific bodies which are in correspondence with all the learned societies of Europe. The government has sent out circumnavigators, who have made discoveries in remote regions of the globe. St. Petersburgh contains museums of art and literature ; some of the first specimens of sculpture and painting are to be seen in its public halls ; its public libraries contain twice as many volumes as those of London ; and the best collection of Chinese, Japanese, and Mongol books are to be found on their shelves. All the decencies and even elegancies of life, observable in Paris or London, are found to prevail over this northern metropolis ; and there is nothing in the streets (unless it be the costume of the people, necessary to meet the exigencies of the climate) to remind the eye of the traveller that he is not in one of the more western Christian capitals.

We may fairly assume that, were Russia to seize upon the capital of Turkey, the consequences would not at least be less favourable to humanity and civilization than those which succeeded to her conquests on the Gulf of Finland a century ago. The seraglio of the Sultan would be once more converted into the palace of a Christian monarch ; the lasciviousness of the harem would disappear at the presence of his Christian empress ; those walls which now resound only to the voice of the eunuch and the slave, and witness nothing but deeds of guilt and dishonour, would then echo the footsteps of travellers and the voices of men of learning, or behold the assemblage of high-souled and beautiful women, of exalted birth and rare accomplishments, the virtuous companions of ambassadors, tourists, and merchants, from all the capitals of Europe. We may fairly and reasonably assume that such consequences would follow the conquest of Constantinople : and can any one doubt that, if the government of St. Petersburg were transferred to the shores of the Bosphorus, a splendid and substantial European city would, in less than twenty years, spring up, in the place of those huts which now constitute the capital of Turkey?—that noble public buildings would arise, learned societies flourish, and the arts prosper?—that, from its natural beauties and advantages, Constantinople would become an attractive resort for civilized Europeans?—that the Christian religion, operating instantly upon the laws and institutions of the country, would ameliorate the condition of its people?—that the slave market which is now polluting the Ottoman capital centuries after the odious traffic has been banished from the soil of Christian Europe, would be abolished?—that the demoralising and unnatural law of polygamy, under which the fairest portion of the creation becomes an object of brutal lust and an article of daily traffic, would be discountenanced? —and that the plague, no longer fostered by the filth and indolence of the people, would cease to ravage countries placed in the healthiest latitudes and blessed with the finest climate in the world? Can any rational mind doubt that these changes would follow from the occupation of Constantinople by Russia, every one of which, so far as the difference in the cases permitted, has already been realised more than a century in St. Petersburg? But the interests of England, it is alleged, would be endangered by such changes. We deny that the progress of improvement and the advance of civilization can be inimical to the welfare of Great Britain. To assert that *we*, a commercial and manufacturing people, have an interest in retaining the fairest regions in Europe in barbarism and ignorance—that *we* are benefited because poverty, slavery, polygamy, and the plague abound in Turkey—is a fallacy too gross even for refutation.

One of the greatest dangers apprehended (for we set out with promising to answer the popular objections to the aggrandisement of Russia in this quarter) is, from the injury which would be inflicted upon our trade; which trade, exclusively of that portion of our nominal exports to Turkey which really goes to Persia, does not much exceed half a million yearly, an amount so contemptible when we recollect the population, magnitude, and natural fertility of that empire, that it might safely be predicted, under no possible form of government could it be diminished. But Russia is said, by the panegyrists of Turkey, to be an anti-commercial country. We have already seen that, to Russian influence we are indebted for the liberation of the Black Sea from the thraldom in which it had been held, by Turkish jealousy, for three hundred years. If, however, we would judge of the probable conduct of that people after the conquest of Constantinople, we must appeal to the experience which they have given us of their commercial policy at St. Petersburg. The first Dutch merchant vessel (whose captain was welcomed with honours and loaded with presents by Peter the Great) entered that harbour in 1703 ; and, at the present time, fifteen hundred vessels clear out annually from the capital of Russia for all parts of the world. The internal navigation of this vast empire has been improved, with a patience and perseverance, in the last century, which, bearing in mind the impediments of climate and soil, are deserving our astonishment and admiration, and which contrasts strangely with the supineness of that Mahometan people whose habits are, according to some writers, so favourable to trade, but in whose country not one furlong of canal or navigable stream, the labour of Turkish hands, has been produced in upwards of three hundred years! Three great lines of navigation, one of them 1,400 miles long, extend through the interior of Russia, by which the waters of the Baltic, the Caspian, and the Black Sea are brought into connection; and by which channels the provinces of the Volga, the plains of the Ukraine, and the forests and mines of Siberia, transmit their products to the markets of Moscow and St. Petersburg.* Much as may with truth be alleged against the lust for aggrandizement with which Russian counsels have been actuated, yet, if we examine, we shall find that it is by the love of improvement—the security given, by laws, to life and property—but, above all, owing to the encouragement afforded to commerce—that this empire has, more than by conquest, been brought forth from her frozen regions, to hold a first rank among the nations of Europe.

The laws for the encouragement of trade are direct and important; and their tendency is to destroy the privileges of the nobles, by raising up a middle class precisely in the same way by which our own Plantagenets countervailed the powers of the barons. Every Russian, carrying on trade, must be a burgher, and a registered member of a guild or company; and of these guilds there are three ranks, according to the capitals of the members :—

10 to 50,000 roubles† entitles to foreign commerce, exempts from corporal punishment, and qualifies to drive about in a carriage and pair.

5 to 10,000 roubles, the members of this guild are confined to inland trade.

1 to 5,000 roubles includes petty shopkeepers.

Besides these guilds for merchants, the porters of the large towns associate together in bodies, called

---

* Boats may, we are told, go from St. Petersburg to the Caspian Sea without unloading.

† A rouble is about 10½d.

artels, resembling, in some respects, the company of wine coopers in London, for the purpose of guaranteeing persons employing one of them from any loss or damage to his goods. Now, in a country, however far removed from a state of freedom and civilization (*and we maintain that, in these respects, the condition of Russia is in arrear of all other Christian states*), where laws such as these exist, for encouraging industry, conferring privileges upon traders, and doing honour to the accumulation of capital—in that country prodigious strides have been already taken on the only true path to enlightenment and liberty. *On this path the Turks have disdained to advance a single step.* Here we have at one glance the distinctive characters of the Turkish and Russian, the Sclavonic and Mongolian races—the former unchanging and stationary, the latter progressing and imitative. The very stringent laws which Russia has passed against the importation of our fabrics are indications of the same variety of character, evincing a desire to rival us in mechanical industry; whilst the apathy with which the Turk sees every article of our manufacture enter his ports, without being stimulated to study the construction of a loom or spinning frame, is but another manifestation of his inferior structure of intellect.

To return, then, to the oft-agitated question, as to the danger of our commerce consequent upon the conquest of Constantinople by Russia—are we not justified in assuming that our exports to Turkey would exceed half a million per annum if that fertile region were possessed by a nation governed under laws for the fostering of trade, such as we have just described? Some persons argue, indeed, that, although the productive industry of those countries would augment under such supposed circumstances, still, so great is the enmity of the Russians towards England, that we should be excluded from all participation in its increase. But how stands the case if we appeal to the policy of that people, as already experienced, and find that—notwithstanding that our own tariff at this time interposes a duty of 100 per cent. against the two staple articles of Russian produce, timber and corn—the amount of trade carried on between Great Britain and St. Petersburg is equal to that of the latter with all the rest of the world together; for, of the 1,500 vessels clearing annually from that port, 750 are British? But it is contended that, if Russia were put into possession of the Turkish provinces, she would possess, within her own limits, such a command of all the natural products as might enable her to close the Hellespont against the world, and begin a Japanese system of commercial policy. To this we reply, that commerce cannot, in the present day, turn hermit. It will not answer for a people to try, in the words of Sheridan, to get "an atmosphere and a sun of its own." Nay, better still—no country can carry on great financial transactions except through the medium of England. We are told by Mr. Rothschild, in his evidence before the legislature, that London is the metropolis of the moneyed world; that no large commercial operations can possibly be carried on, but they must be, more or less, under the influence of this common centre of the financial system, round which the less affluent states, like the humbler orbs of the solar creation, revolve, and from whence they must be content to borrow lustre and nourishment. Supposing, indeed, that Russia were in possession of Turkey, and should commence a system of non-intercourse (we are under the necessity of making these whimsical suppositions in order to reply to grounds of argument which are actually advanced every day by *grave* writers upon this question), could she carry on those extensive manufactures which some people predict, without deriving a supply of raw ingredients from other countries? It will suffice on this head if we observe, that, to enable any one of our manufacturers to conduct the simplest branch of his mechanical and chemical industry it is requisite that he be duly supplied with materials, the growth of every corner of the globe. The commonest printed calico, worn by the poorest peasant's wife, is the united product of the four quarters of the earth : the cotton of America, the indigo of Asia, the gum of Africa, and the madder of Europe, must all be brought from those remote regions, and be made to combine with fifty other as apparently heterogeneous commodities, by ingenious arts and processes, the results of ten thousand philosophical experiments, and all to produce a rustic's gown-piece! Whilst such are the exigencies of manufacturing industry, binding us in abject dependence upon all the countries of the earth, may we not hope that freedom of commerce, and an exemption from warfare, will be the inevitable fruits of the future growth of that mechanical and chemical improvement, the *germ* of which has only been planted in our day ? Need we add one word to prove that Russia could not—unless she were to discover another chemistry which should wholly alter the properties of matter —at the same time seclude herself from the trade of the rest of the world, and become a rich and great manufacturing or commercial nation? Wherever a country is found to favour foreign commerce, whether it be the United States, Russia, Holland, China, or Brazil (we speak only of commercial nations, and, of course, do not include France), it may infallibly be assumed, that England partakes more largely of the advantages of that traffic than any other state ; and the same rule will continue to apply to the *increase* of the commerce of the world, in whatever quarter it may be, so long as the British people are distinguished by their industry, energy, and ingenuity ; and provided that their rulers shall keep pace in wise reforms and severe economy with the governments of their rivals. It follows, then, that, with reference to trade, there can be no ground of apprehension from Russia. If that people were to attempt to exclude all foreign traffic, they would enter at once upon the high road to barbarism, from which career there is no danger threatened to rich and civilized nations ; if, on the other hand, that state continued to pursue a system favourable to foreign trade, then England would be found at Constantinople, as she has already been at St. Petersburg, reaping the greatest harvest of riches and power from the augmentation of Russian imports.

By far the greater proportion of the writers and speakers upon the subject of the power of Russia either do not understand, or lose sight of, the all-important question, What is the true source of national greatness ? The path by which alone modern empires can hope to rise to supreme power and grandeur (would that we could impress this sentiment upon the mind of every statesman in Europe !) is that of labour and improvement. They who, pointing to the chart of Russia, shudder at her expanse of impenetrable forests, her wastes of eternal snow, her howling wildernesses, frowning mountains, and solitary rivers ; or they who stand aghast at her boundless extent of fertile but uncultivated steppes, her millions of serfs, and her towns, the abodes of poverty and filth—know nothing of the true origin, in modern and future times, of national power and greatness. This question admits of an appropriate illustration, by putting the names of a couple of heroes of Russian aggression and violence in contrast with two of their contemporaries, the champions of improvement in England. At the very period when Potemkin and Suwarrow were engaged in effecting their important Russian conquests in Poland and the Crimea, andwhilst those monsters of carnage were filling the world with the lustre of their fame, and lighting up one-half of Europe with the conflagrations of war, two obscure individuals, the one an optician, and the other a barber, both equally disregarded by the chroniclers of the day, were quietly gaining victories in the realms of science which have produced a more abundant harvest of wealth and power to their native country than has been acquired by all the wars of Russia during the last two centuries. Those illustrious commanders in the war of improvement, Watt and Arkwright, with a band of subalterns—the thousand ingenious and practical discoverers who have followed in their train—have, with their armies of artisans, conferred a power and consequence upon England, springing from successive triumphs in the physical sciences and the mechanical arts, and wholly independent of territorial increase, compared with which all that she owes to the evanescent exploits of her warrior heroes sinks into insignificance and obscurity. If we look into futurity, and speculate upon the probable career of one of these inventions, may we not with safety predict that the steam engine—the perfecting of which belongs to our own age, and which even now is exerting an influence in the four quarters of the globe—will at no distant day produce moral and physical changes, all over the world, of a magnitude and permanency surpassing the effects of all the wars and conquests which have convulsed mankind since the beginning of time. England owes to the peaceful exploits of Watt and Arkwright, and not to the deeds of Nelson and Wellington, her commerce, which now extends to every corner of the earth, and which casts into comparative obscurity, by the grandeur and extent of its operations, the peddling ventures of Tyre, Carthage, and Venice, confined within the limits of an inland sea.

If we were to trace, step by step, the opposite careers of aggrandizement—to which we can only thus hastily glance—of England, pursuing the march of improvement within the area of four of her counties, by exploring the recesses of her mines, by constructing canals, docks, and railroads, by her mechanical inventions, and by the patience and ingenuity of her manufacturers in adapting their fabrics to meet the varying wants and tastes of every habitable latitude of the earth's surface; and of Russia, adhering to her policy of territorial conquests, by despoiling of provinces, the empires of Turkey, Persia, and Sweden, by subjugating in unwilling bondage the natives of Georgia and Circassia, and by seizing with robber hand the soil of Poland—if we were to trace these opposite careers of aggrandizement, what should we find to be the relative consquences to these two empires? England, with her steam engine and spinning frame, has erected the standard of improvement, around which every nation of the world has already prepared to rally; she has, by the magic of her machinery, united for ever two remote hemispheres in the bonds of peace, by placing Europe and America in absolute and inextricable dependence on each other; England's industrious classes, through the energy of their commercial enterprise, are at this moment influencing the civilization of the whole world, by stimulating the labour, exiting the curiosity, and promoting the taste for refinement of barbarous communities, and, above all, by acquiring and teaching to surrounding nations the beneficent attachment to peace. Such are the moral effects of improvement in Britain, against which Russia can oppose comparatively little but the example of violence, to which humanity points as a beacon to warn society from evil. And if we refer to the physical effects—if, for the sake of convincing minds which do not recognise the far more potent moral influences, we descend to a comparison of mere brute forces—we find still greater superiority resulting from ingenuity and labour. The manufacturing districts alone—even the four counties of England, comprising Lancashire, Yorkshire, Cheshire, and Staffordshire—could, at any moment, by means of the wealth drawn, by the skill and industry of its population, from the natural resources of this comparative speck of territory, combat with success the whole Russian Empire! Liverpool and Hull, with their navies, and Manchester, Leeds, and Birmingham, with their capitals, could blockade, within the the waters of Cronstadt, the entire Russian marine, and annihilate the commerce of St. Petersburgh. And,

C

further, if we suppose that, during the next thirty years, Russia, adhering to her system of territorial aggrandizement, were to swallow up successively her neighbours, Persia and Turkey, whilst England, which we have imagined to comprise only the area of four counties, still persevered in her present career of mechanical ingenuity, the relative forces would, at the end of that time, yet be more greatly in favour of the peaceful and industrious empire. This mere speck on the ocean—without colonies, which are but the costly appendage* of an aristocratic government—without wars, which have ever been but another aristocratic mode of plundering and oppressing commerce—would, with only a few hundred square leagues of surface, by means of the wealth which, by her arts and industry, she had accumulated, be the arbitress of the destiny of Russia, with its millions of square miles of territory. Liverpool and Hull, with their thousands of vessels, would be in a condition to dictate laws to the possessors of one-fourth part of the surface of the globe : they would then be enabled to blockade Russia in the Sea of Marmora, as they could now do in the Gulf of Finland—to deny her the freedom of the seas—to deprive her proud nobles of every foreign commodity and luxury, and degrade them, amidst their thousands of serfs, to the barbarous state of their ancestors of the ancient Rousniacs—and to confine her Czar in his splendid prison of

---

* Some people contend that our colonies are profitable to us, because they consume our manufactures ; although it is notorious that they do not buy a single commodity from us which they could procure cheaper elsewhere, whilst we take frequently articles from them of an inferior quality, and at a dearer rate than we could purchase at from other countries. But what do the advocates of the present system say to the fact that we are at this moment paying thirty per cent. more for the colonial productions consumed in our houses than is paid for similar articles, *procured from our own colonies, too*, by the people of the Continent? A workman in London, an artizan in Manchester, or a farmer of Wales, buys his Jamaica sugar and coffee thirty per cent. dearer than the native of Switzerland or America, perhaps five hundred miles distant from a port, and whose governments never owned a colony ! But, it will be said, this is necessary taxation to meet the interest of the debt. And what have we to show for the national debt but our colonies ?

Constantinople!*   If such are the miracles of the mind, such the superiority of improvement over the efforts of brute force and violence, is not the writer of these pages justified in calling the attention of his countrymen else-where † to the progress of another people, whose rapid adoption of the discoveries of the age, whose mechanical skill and unrivalled industry in all the arts of life—as exemplified in their thousands of miles of railroads, their hundreds of steam-boats, their ship-building, manufacturing, patent inventions—whose system of universal instruction, and, above all, whose inveterate attachment to peace—all proclaim America, by her com-petition in improvements, to be destined to affect more vitally than Russia, by her aggrandizement of territory, the future interests of Great Britain?

If then, England, by promoting the peaceful industry of her population, is pursuing a course which shall con-duct her to a far higher point of moral and physical power than Russia can hope to reach by the opposite

---

* The amount of our exports of cotton goods, of which industry Man-chester is the centre, is double that of the exports of every kind from all the Russian Empire ; the shipping entering Liverpool annually exceeds the tonnage of St. Petersburgh eightfold !   These facts which we can only thus allude to with epigrammatic brevity, convey forcibly to the reflecting mind an impression of the mighty influence which now slumbers in the possession of the commercial and manufacturing portions of the community ; how little they understand the extent of their power may be acknowledged when we recollect that this great and independent order of society (for the manufacturing interest of England is, from the nature of its position with reference to foreign states, more independent of British agriculture than the latter is of it) is deprived of the just reward of its ingenious labour by the tyranny of the corn-laws ; that it possesses no representation, and conse-quently no direct influence, in *one* of the Houses of Parliament—the mem-bers of which, to a man, are interested in the manufacture and high price of food ; and that it still lies under the stigma of feudal laws, that confer rights, privileges, and exemptions upon landed possessions, which are denied to personal property.

† Since the publication of " England, Ireland, and America," the author has had an opportunity of visiting the United States, and of taking a hasty glance of the American people ; and his ocular experience of the country has confirmed him in the views he put forth in that pamphlet. Looking to the natural endowments of the North American continent—as

career of war and conquest, we must seek for some other motive than that of danger to ourselves, for the hostilities in which we are urged, by so many writers and speakers, to engage with that northern people.

The great grievance, indeed, with us, is one which, all things borne in remembrance, displays quite as much naïveté in the character of the British people as is

superior to Europe as the latter is to Africa—with an almost immeasurable extent of river navigation—its boundless expanse of the most fertile soil in the world, and its inexhaustible mines of coal, iron, lead, &c.—looking at these, and remembering the quality and position of a people universally instructed and perfectly free, and possessing, as a consequence of these, a new-born energy and vitality very far surpassing the character of any nation of the old world—the writer reiterates the moral of his former work, by declaring his conviction that it is from the west, rather than from the east, that danger to the supremacy of Great Britain is to be apprehended ;—that it is from the silent and peaceful rivalry of American commerce, the growth of its manufactures, its rapid progress in internal improvements, the superior education of its people, and their economical and pacific government—that it is from these, and not from the barbarous policy or the impoverishing armaments of Russia, that the grandeur of our commercial and national prosperity is endangered. *And the writer stakes his reputation upon the prediction, that, in less than twenty years, this will be the sentiment of the people of England generally; and that the same conviction will be forced upon the government of the country.*

The writer has been surprised at the little knowledge that exists here with respect to the mineral resources of America. Few are aware that in nothing does that country surpass Europe so much as in its rich beds of coal. By a government survey of the State of Pennsylvania, it appears that it contains twenty thousand square miles of coal, with iron in proportion. This in one State only ! whilst the whole of the Mississippi valley is more or less enriched with this invaluable combustible. Several of his neighbours have been astonished by the inspection of a specimen of bituminous coal, which the writer procured from a pit at Brownsville, on the Monongahela river, above Pittsburgh, and which is pronounced equal to the very best qualities produced from the mines in Yorkshire. The mode of working the pits is, to drive an adit into the sloping banks of the navigable rivers ; and, at a few yards' distance, the coal stratum is usually found, six feet in thickness ; and, as the miner is always enabled to work in an upright posture, one man will frequently produce as much as 100 loads a day. The steam-boat in which the author went from Brownsville to Pittsburgh, stopped at one of those pits' mouths, and took in a supply of fuel, which was charged at the rate of about three farthings a bushel. These are facts which bear more directly upon the future destinies of this country, than the marriages of crowned heads in Portugal, the movements of savage forces in Russia, and similar proceedings, to which we attach so much importance.

consistent with a moderate share of self-knowledge. The Russians are accused by *us* of being an aggrandizing people! From the day of Pultowa down to the time of the passage of the Balkan—say the orators, journalists, reviewers, and authors—the government of St. Petersburgh has been incessantly addicted to picking and stealing. But, in the meantime, has England been idle? If, during the last century, Russia has plundered Sweden, Poland, Turkey, and Persia, until she has grown unwieldy with the extent of her spoils, Great Britain has, in the same period, robbed—no, that would be an unpolite phrase — "*has enlarged the bounds of his Majesty's dominions*" at the expense of France, Holland, and Spain. It would be false logic, and just as unsound morality, to allow the Muscovite to justify his derelictions of honesty by an appeal to our example ; but surely we, who are staggering under the embarrassing weight of our colonies, with one foot upon the rock of Gibraltar and the other at the Cape of Good Hope— with Canada, Australia, and the peninsula of India, forming, Cerberus-like, the heads of our monstrous empire—and with the hundred minor acquisitions scattered so widely over the earth's surface as to present an unanswerable proof of our wholesome appetite for boundless dominion—surely *we* are not exactly the nation to preach homilies to other people in favour of the national observance of the eighth commandment!* If *we* find all these possessions to be burdensome, rather than profitable—if, in common with all marauders, *we* discover, by experience, that the acquisitions of fraud or violence confer nothing but disappointment and loss—

* *Extract from Mr. T. Attwood's speech, House of Commons, July 9, 1833.*—" The House will recollect that, for two centuries, Russia has been gradually encroaching upon the territories of all her neighbours ; for the last 150 years her progress has been general on all sides—east, west, north, and south. A few years ago, she attacked Sweden and seized upon Finland. Then she attacked Persia, and added some most important provinces to her empire in the south. Not content with this, she appropriated, in 1792, a great part of Poland ; and it is but lately she has

we shall not improve our case by going to war to prevent
Russia pursuing the same course, which will inevitably
conduct her to a similar fate, where the same retribution,
which will ever accompany an infringement of the moral
laws, awaits her. England and Russia, in the act of scold-
ing each other on the reciprocal accusation of unjust aggrandizement, present an appearance so ludicrous that it
forcibly recalls to our recollection the quarrel between
the two worthies of the Beggars' Opera, the termination
of which scene we recommend to the imitation of the
diplomatists of the two Courts.   Like Lockit and
Peachum, the British lion and the Russian bear, instead
of tearing one another, had better hug and be friends—
" Brother *bruin*, brother *bruin*, we are both in the wrong."

Lord Dudley Stuart (whose zeal, we fear, without
knowledge, upon the subject of Poland, and whose prejudice against Russia, have led him to occupy so much of the
public time, uselessly, upon the question before us), in the
course of his long speech in the House of Commons (Feb-
ruary 19th), upon introducing the subject of Russian encroachments, dwelt, at considerable length, upon the lust
of aggrandizement, by which he argued that the government of St. Petersburgh was so peculiarly distinguished ;
and he brought forward, at considerable cost of labour,
details of its successive conquests of territory during the
last century.   Where the human mind is swayed by any
passion, of however amiable a nature, or where the feelings are allowed to predominate over the reason, in
investigating a subject which appeals only to the under-
standing, it will generally happen that the judgment is
defective.   We attribute to the well-known fervour of

attacked Turkey.   Thus, for years, she has gone on in her course of
aggrandizement, in defiance of the laws of God and man !"   If for Sweden,
Persia, and Poland, we substitute France, Spain, and Holland, and if,
instead of Turkey, we put the Burmese empire, how admirably the above
description would apply to another nation, of whose unprofitable aggran-
dizements in Europe, Asia, Africa, and America, Mr. Attwood may read a
few particulars in Mr. Montgomery Martin's "History of the British
Colonies"—five volumes, octavo !

Lord Stuart's sentiments upon Russia and Poland, the circumstance that, during the fortnight which he must have employed in collecting the dates of the several treaties by which the former empire has wrested its possessions from neighbouring states, the thought never once occurred to him—a reflection which would have entered the head of almost any other man of sense, who sat down coolly to consider the subject—that, during the last hundred years, England has, for every square league of territory annexed to Russia, *by force, violence, or fraud, appropriated to herself three.* Such would have been the reflection which flashed across the mind of a statesman who sat down, *dispassionately*, to investigate the subject of Russian policy; and it must have prevented him, by the consciousness of the egotism and arrogance—nay, the downright effrontery * of such a course—from bringing an accusation against another people which recoils with threefold † criminality upon ourselves. Nor, if we were to enter upon a comparison of the cases, should we find that the *means* whereby Great Britain has augmented her possessions, are a whit less reprehensible than those which have been resorted to by the northern power for a similar purpose. If the English writer calls down indignation upon the conquerors of the Ukraine, Finland, and the

---

* We allude to the nation—the epithet cannot be applied to his lordship.

† We speak after due investigation and calculation, and not at random, when we allege that England has acquired three times as much territory as Russia during the last century. The Cape is computed at half a million of square miles, Canada at half as much more, India and New Holland will be found each with an area almost as large as that of the cultivable portion of Europe; not to mention other acquisitions too numerous to be described within the limits of a pamphlet!

Progressive augmentation of the Russian Empire :—

		Sq miles.	Population.
At the accession of Peter I. .	. .	1689, 2,980,000	15,000,000
At his death	.	1725, 3,150,000	20,000,000
At the accession of Catherine II. .	.	1763, 3,700,000	25,000,000
At her death . . .	.	1796, 3,850,000	36,000,000
At the death of Alexander .	.	1825, 4,250,000	58,000,000

—*Malte Brun's Geography*, vol. vi., p. 622.

Crimea, may not Russian historians conjure up equally painful reminiscences upon the subjects of Gibraltar, the Cape, and Hindostan? Every one conversant with the history of the last century, will remember that England has, during almost all that period, maintained an ascendency at sea; and colonies, which were in times past regarded as the chief source of our wealth and power, being pretty generally the fruits of every succeeding war, the nation fell into a passion for conquest, under the delusive impression that those distant dependencies were, in spite of the debt contracted in seizing them, profitable acquisitions to the mother country. Hence the British Government was always eager for hostilities, the moment an excuse presented itself, with one of the maritime continental states, possessing colonies; and of the several conflicts in which we have been involved since the peace of Ryswick, at least three out of four have been consequent upon declarations of war made by England.* Russia, on the contrary, has been nearly surrounded by the territory of barbarous nations, one of

---

* The policy of England has been aggressive at all times; but we are far from exulting in the fact of having always dealt the first blow, as Mr. Thomas Attwood of Birmingham would wish us to do, when he tells us, exultingly, in the House of Commons, whilst speaking of Russia—(*See Mirror of Parliament*, 1833, *p.* 2874.)—" We, the people of England, who have never know what fear is; who have been accustomed, for seven hundred years, to give a blow first and to receive an apology afterwards; we, who have borne the British lion triumphant through every quarter of the world, and are now forced to submit to insults from this base and brutal, and this in reality weak power—a power which, from its mere physical force, contrives, like a great bully, to intimidate the moral strength of Europe!" Now, putting aside the exquisitely ludicrous charge of bullying, alleged against Russia by one who boasts that, for seven hundred years, we have "struck the first blow," and which reminds us of the scene between Sir Anthony Absolute and his "insolent, overbearing" son, Jack; we have here a specimen of that sort of sentiment which horses or buffaloes, if they could make speeches, might very properly indulge in, but which is derogatory to the rank of reasoning beings, who possess intellectual faculties in lieu of hoofs and horns.

Mr. Attwood is an advocate for war and paper money—*the curse and scourge of the working classes!* What do the Birmingham mechanics say to the following picture of the effects of the last war upon the prosperity of

which*—*by the very nature of its institutions warlike and aggressive*—was, up to the middle of the last century, prompted by a consciousness of strength, and, since then, by a haughty ignorance of its degeneracy, to court hostilities with its neighbours ; and the consequence of this and other causes is, that, in the majority of cases, where Russia has been engaged in conflicts with her neighbours, she will be found to have had a war of self-defence for her justification.   If such are the facts—if England has, for the sake of the spoil which would accrue to her superiority of naval strength, provoked war, with all its horrors, from weak and unwilling enemies, whilst Russia, on the contrary, with ill-defined boundaries, has been called upon to repel the attacks of fierce and lawless nations—surely, we must admit, unless pitiably blind by national vanity, that the gain (if such there be) resulting from these contentions, is not less unholy in the former than the latter case ; and that the title by which the sovereign of St. Petersburgh holds his conquered possessions is just as good, at least, as that

their town?   The same results would follow a like cause, should a war be entered into, to gratify their favourite representative.

Extract from Mr. Grey's (now Lord Grey) speech on the state of the nation, March 25, 1801.—See Hansard's Parliamentary History, vol. xxxv., p. 1064.

" I come now to speak of the internal state of the country.   Two hundred and seventy millions have been added to our national debt, exclusive of imperial and other loans, and of the reduction effected by the sinking fund ; and yet we are told by the ex-ministers that they leave the country in a flourishing situation !   I ask any man whether, from diminished comforts or from positive distress, he does not feel this declaration an insult ? Ask the ruined manufacturers of Yorkshire, Manchester, and Birmingham ; ask the starving inhabitants of London and Westminster.   In some parts of Yorkshire, formerly the most flourishing, it appears, from an authentic paper which I hold in my hand, that the poor-rates have increased from £522 to £6,000 a year ; though the whole rack-rent of the parish does not exceed £5,600.   *In Birmingham, I know from undoubted authority, there are near 11,000 persons who receive parochial relief, though the whole number of the inhabitants cannot exceed 80,000—and this of a town reckoned one of the most prosperous in England.*"

* Turkey.

by which the government of St. James's asserts the
right to ours. In the case of Poland, to which we shall
again have to recur by and by, there was, indeed,
a better title than that of the sword, but which, amidst
the clamour of fine sentiments, palmed by philanthropic
authors and speakers upon the much abused public mind,
about Russian aggression in that quarter, has never, we
believe, been mentioned by any orator, reviewer, or
newspaper writer of the present day. The " Republic of
Poland " (we quote the words of Malte Brun) " had been
chiefly composed of provinces wrested from Russia, or
from the Great Dukes of Galitch, Vladimir, Volynski,
Polotzk, and particularly Kiow, by Boleslas the Victorious,
Casimir the Great, Kings of Poland, and by Gedimir,
Great Duke of Lithuania. Thus, the nobles were the
only persons interested in the defence of provinces, whose
inhabitants were estranged from the Poles, although they
had remained under their government from the time of
the conquest. All the peasants of Podolia and Volhynia,
were Rousniacs, or Little Russians, ignorant of the language or customs of Poland, which may partly account
for the success of the Russians in their invasions of the
Polish republic. The Poles, who were persecuted by
intolerant Catholic Priests, who disregarded the consti-
tutions of the Polish diet, abandoned their lords without
reluctance, and received willingly their countrymen, the
Russian soldiers, who spoke the same dialect as themselves. The division of Poland was, on the part of
Russia, not so much a lawless invasion as an act of
reprisal on former invaders. Had this leading historical
fact been explained in the Russian manifesto, which
was published in 1772, so much obloquy might not have
been attached to the conduct of that people."

Leaving, however, the question of title—which, whatever may be the conflicting opinions of moralists and
legists, is, in the case of national tenures, usually decided
according to the *power* of the possessor to hold in fee—
we shall be next reminded of the great benefits which

British conquests have conferred upon remote and un-civilized nations, particularly in the example of India; and we shall be called upon to show in what manner Russia has compensated for her violent seizures of inde-pendent territory, by any similar amelioration of the condition of its people. Before doing so, we shall pre-mise that we do not offer it as a justification of the policy of Russia. If, by chance, the plunderer makes good use of his spoil, that is not a vindication of robbery; and because the serf of Poland, the savage of Georgia, and the ryot of Bengal, enjoy better laws under the sway of Russia and Great Britain, than they formerly pos-sessed beneath their own governments—to argue that, therefore, these two powers stand morally justified in having subjugated, with fire and sword, those three less civilized states, would be to contend that America, in-stead of contenting herself with imparting improvements to the unenlightened communities of Europe, by the peaceful but irresistible means of her high example, is warranted in invading Naples or Spain, for the purpose of rescuing their people from the thraldom of monarchy, or marching to Rome, and, in place of the Pope, in-stalling a President in the palace of the Vatican!* It is, then, with no view to the justification of war and violence, but solely for the purpose of answering, by a few facts of unquestionable authenticity, those spurious appeals to our sympathies, based upon the false assump-tion of Russian aggrandizement being but another term for the spread of barbarism and the extinction of

* Yet there are perverse and purblind moralists, who can see proofs of God's interposition in every atrocious crime that happens, in its conse-quences, to carry some alloy of good ; which merely proves that the great Ruler of the universe has, in *spite* of us, set His fiat against the predominancy of evil. A clergyman—we believe, Dr. Buchanan—of high attainments and strict evangelical doctrines, who passed many years in India, proposed a prize essay, on his return to England, *as to the probable designs of Providence in placing the Indian Empire in the hands of Great Britain !* This, from a contemporary of Warren Hastings, is little less blasphemous than the *Te Deums* sung by Catherine, for the victories of Ismail and Warsaw.

freedom and civilization, that we glance at the proofs which
are afforded in every direction, of the vast moral, political, and commercial advantages that have been bestowed
upon the countries annexed by conquest to that empire.

The writers who have attempted to lead public
opinion upon the subject, have not scrupled to claim the
interposition of our government with Russia, for the purpose of restoring to *freedom* and *independence* those Cau-
casian tribes to which we have before alluded, as having
fallen under the partial dominion of Russia. Their pre-
vious state of freedom may be appreciated, when we
recollect that, within our own time, a fierce war was waged
between the most powerful of these nations* and the
Turks, in consequence of their having refused to continue
to supply the harems of the latter with a customary
annual tribute of the handsomest of their daughters;
offering, however, at the same time, in lieu, a yearly con-
tribution in money. We have already alluded to the
emancipating influence of Russian intervention over the
commerce of the Black Sea, the only channel by which
the civilizing intercourse with commercial nations can
extend to these unenlightened regions; and we have
been told, by the very highest authority,† that their
trade, agriculture, and social improvement, already attest
the beneficent effects of this improved policy. The following extract from a work ‡ of great and deserved
reputation, gives the most recent information upon the
countries under consideration; and it conveys, perhaps,
all that could be said upon the effects of Russian aggrandizement in these quarters:—"The southern declivity of
these mountains is highly fertile, abounding in forests
and fountains, orchards, vineyards, corn-fields, and pastures in rich variety. Grapes, chestnuts, figs, &c., grow
spontaneously in these countries; as well as grain of

* The Georgians.
† M'Culloch—Commercial Dictionary, vii., p. 1108.
‡ Encyclopædia Britannica, new edition, now publishing, vol. vi., p. 250
—art. Caucasus.

every description—rice, cotton, hemp, &c. But the inhabitants are barbarous and indolent. They consist of mountain tribes, remarkably ferocious, whose delight is in war, and with whom robbery is a hereditary trade ; and their practice is to descend from their fastnesses and to sweep everything away from the neighbouring plains— not only grain and cattle, but men, women, and children, who are carried into captivity. The names of the different tribes are, the Georgians, Abassians, Lesghians, Ossetes, Circassians, Taschkents, Khists, Ingooshes, Charabulaks, Tartars, Armenians, Jews, and in some parts wandering Arabs. They are mostly barbarous in their habits, and idolatrous in their religion, worshipping stars, mountains, rocks, and trees. There are among them Greek and Armenian Christians, Mahometans, and Jews. Several of the tribes, particularly the Circassians and Georgians, are accounted the handsomest people in the world ; and the females are much sought after by the eastern monarchs to be immured in their harems. The inhabitants amount to about 900,000, who are partly ruled by petty sovereigns, and partly by their seniors. The most famous are the Lesghians, who inhabit the eastern regions, and, living by plunder, are the terror of the Armenians, Persians, Turks, and Georgians. Their sole occupation is war, and their services can at any time be purchased by every prince in the neighbourhood, for a supply of provisions and a few silver roubles. *Since the extension of the Russian empire in this quarter, many of these mountain tribes have been restrained in their predatory habits. Under the iron rule of that powerful state, they have been taught to tremble and obey ; military posts have been dispersed over the country, fortresses have been erected, towns have arisen, and commerce and agriculture begin slowly to supplant the barbarous pursuits of war and plunder, in which these mountain tribes have been hitherto engaged.** But the work of civilization in these

* Yet the most active and persevering assailant of Russia, a writer to whom we alluded in the beginning of this pamphlet, does not scruple to

wild regions is still slow; it is difficult to reclaim the people from their long-settled habits of violence and disorder; and it would not be safe for any traveller to pass alone through these countries, where he would be exposed to robbery and murder."

Another ground of ceaseless jealousy, on the part of our philo-Turkish and Russo-maniac writers, has been discovered in the recent intervention of the Russian diplomatists in the affairs of Wallachia and Moldavia. The condition of these two Christian provinces, situated on the right bank of the Danube, and so frequently the scenes of desolating wars between Turkey and her neighbours, has been perhaps more pitiably deplorable than the lot of any other portion of this misgoverned empire. The hospodars or governors of Moldavia and Wallachia were changed every year at the will of the Sultan, and each brought a fresh retinue of greedy dependants, armed with absolute power, to prey upon the defenceless inhabitants. These appointments, as is the case now with every pachalick, were openly sold at Constantinople to the highest bidder; and the hospodars were left to recover from their subjects the price of the purchase, to pay an annual tribute to the Porte, which was usually levied in kind, giving scope for the most arbitrary exactions; and, besides, appease the favourites at court, who might otherwise intrigue against them. Need we be surprised that, under such a state of things, the population decreased, agriculture was neglected, and commerce and the arts of civilized existence were unknown in the finest countries of the world? Not more than one-sixth* part of the land of Wallachia is at

invoke the aid of these hordes against their present rulers :—" The Georgian provinces would instantly throw off the yoke; even the Wallachians, Moldavians, and Bessarabians, would join in the general impulse; the millions of brave and independent Circassians would pour across the Couban and spread over the Crimea—and where would Russia be?"—*See pamphlet*, "*England, France, Russia, and Turkey.*"

* The clergy, from being exempt from taxation, have become possessed of a third of the soil.

present cultivated ; and Mr. Wilkinson, the late English consul, estimated that, without any extraordinary exertion, the existing population of Wallachia and Moldavia might, if property were secured, raise twice the quantity of corn and double the number of cattle now produced in those provinces. The treaty of 1829, between Russia and Turkey, stipulates that the hospodars shall be elected for life, and that no tribute in kind shall be levied ; it also engages that a qurantine shall be placed on the Danube frontier, thus separating these provinces from the rest of Turkey. This case of intervention is appealed to as a proof of Russian ambition ; and Lord Stuart, in the course of his speech before alluded to, complains that, by this policy, its power is increased in those quarters. Admitting that Russia interferes in behalf of those unhappy countries with no loftier aim than the augmentation of her influence, and that the result will be the separation of the Christian provinces of Moldavia and Wallachia from the rest of the Turkish territory—nay, admitting that this should prove inimical to the interests of England (though the supposition is absurd enough, since whatever tends to advance the civilization, and augment the wealth of any part of the world, must be beneficial in the end to us who are the greatest commercial and manufacturing people)—still the English nation would, we sincerely hope, feel a disinterested gratitude to the power which, by its merciful interposition, has rescued this suffering Christian community from the cruel, remorseless, and harassing grasp of its Mahometan oppressors.

Probably it will not be deemed necessary that we should trace the effects of Russian government over the territories torn at different epochs from the Persian empire ; if, however, we did not feel warranted in assuming that even those of our intelligent readers who may be the most inimical to the power of the Czar, will readily admit the superiority of the organized despotism of St. Petersburgh over the anarchic tyranny of Teheran, we should be prepared to afford proofs, from the works of travellers themselves hostile to Russian interests, of the rapid ameliorations that have succeeded to the extension of this colossal empire in those regions. Still less shall we be called upon to pause to point out the benefits that must ensue from the annexation of the Crimea to the dominions of the Autocrat. Those wandering tribes of Crim Tartars who exchanged, for the service of the Empress Catherine, the barbarous government of the descendants of Genghis Khan, and who received, as the first fruits of a Christian administration, the freedom of the commerce of the world, by the opening of the navigation of the Black Sea, which immediately succeeded to the encroachments of Russia in that quarter, will gradually but certainly acquire the taste for trade ; and, as population increases and towns arise, they will abandon, of necessity, their migratory habits, and become the denizens of civilized society.

We shall, for the sake of brevity, restrict ourselves to the following short passage, from the highest authority that can be consulted, upon the character of Russian policy towards her latest maritime acquisition on the side of the Baltic. " Finland," says Malte Brun, " was averse to the union with Sweden, and has lost none of its privileges by being incorporated with Russia ; it is still governed by Swedish laws ; schools have been established during the last twenty years, and the peasantry are in every respect as well protected as in Sweden," *

* Vol. vi., p. 499, Malte Brun's Geography.

LONDON : CASSELL PETTER & GALPIN, BELLE SAUVAGE WORKS, LUDGATE HILL, E.C.